T0262409

THE

Deliberate Dreamer's

JOURNAL

THE
Deliberate Dreamer's
JOURNAL

Athena Laz

A TarcherPerigee Book

tarcherperigee

an imprint of Penguin Random House LLC
penguinrandomhouse.com

Most TarcherPerigee books are available at special quantity discounts for bulk
purchase for sales promotions, premiums, fund-raising, and educational
needs. Special books or book excerpts also can be created to fit specific needs.
For details, write: SpecialMarkets@penguinrandomhouse.com.

ISBN 9780593421673

Printed in the United States of America
1st Printing

Book design by Lorie Pagnozzi

Deliberate dreamer (noun): A person who dreams consciously and with intention.

WHAT HAVE YOU BEEN

DREAMING OF?

WHAT STORIES ARE YOU WEAVING

NOW, DEAR DREAMER?

AND WHAT WILL YOU DREAM

UP NEXT?

THE GIFT OF YOUR DREAMS

Every night you are given gifts in the form of your dreams. Gifts that reveal the treasures of your interior life, your greatest potential, and even your destiny! Yet dreams are mysterious things. They speak to us in a curious language, one not made of sound and syllable but rather of symbol, image, and metaphor. The more proficient you become with this language, the greater guidance you will receive.

Even more curious and wonderful is that this language is specific to each and every one of us. For example, a dream of a seed may not mean the same thing to you as it does to me. I understand the image of a seed to represent fertile growth as well as being illustrative of things occurring below the surface. A seed, as a symbolic image, reminds me to cultivate patience and nurturance in both my life and relationships. Perhaps when asked what you think a seed represents, you thought of something entirely different. Maybe a memory associated with a seed sprung to the forefront of your mind? Memories and life experiences greatly influence how we interpret dream messages. After all, in the world of dreams, a seed is rarely just a seed.

Now add dream figures into the picture, and dreams become even more delightful! What does it mean when you interact with your ancestors in a dream?

Or a random person from your everyday life who irritates you well beyond your comfort zone? What is the message behind the stories and interactions that you experience nightly? Dreams help to illuminate the heart, mind, and spirit. They also invite us nightly into a conversation with the mystery that weaves all of life together.

For all these reasons, journals are a powerful tool for uncovering the wisdom in dreams. The more you work with your dreams through journaling, the easier it will become for you to understand their transcendent level of symbolic guidance. And as you come to trust and follow this guidance, you will notice how your life changes for the better.

It is equally wonderful to know that journaling in general has been scientifically proven to aid in emotional and mental well-being. This is due to the fact that the very act of writing about your experiences on a daily basis helps you to process your emotions better and therefore experience greater well-being. Not only that, but contemporary research has now proven that journaling helps strengthen immune cells called T lymphocytes! What a wonderful thought: every morning when you journal in this dream book, not only are you potentially strengthening your immune system, but you also are connecting to the majesty that is your inner world!

HOW DREAMS CAN HELP

* They help you decipher inner thoughts and feelings you might not have been conscious of.

* They enhance creativity and well-being.

* They help shed light on unhelpful and long-standing psychological patterns and behaviors so you can change them for the better.

* They help highlight both healthy and unhealthy relationship dynamics.

* They offer creative solutions, often represented by symbols or dream figures that are very hard to ignore or forget!

* They provide a higher perspective, so if you feel like you are stuck in a pervasive problem, really pay attention to your dreams!

* They help you witness your judgment, pain, and separation so you can feel love and compassion instead.

* They show you your own generosity of spirit.

* They help you in transitional times so you feel more supported and guided.

* They highlight inner conflict so that it can be resolved.

HOW TO USE THIS BOOK

This journal was created with you in mind so that you may receive the maximum benefit from your dreams. You will notice that there are a number of pages dedicated to each night's dreams. This has been done very intentionally in order to give you enough room to record and reflect on your dreams comfortably.

There is also space for you to reflect on the following question: *What action am I being guided to take?* This question has been deliberately positioned throughout this journal in order to help you to move beyond interpretation and into the realm of action. Mindful interpretation followed through with cultivated action is the pathway to greater well-being and positive progress. So use your dreams by taking action on the helpful guidance you receive!

You will also notice that following your journaling pages for each night, I have added a checklist for ease and assistance. It can be used in two ways. The first is that upon waking, while you still vividly remember the full aspects of your dream, it's helpful to quickly jot down the key points in the checklist. The key points are the prominent symbols, people, and places that appear in your dream. The process of writing in the checklist helps solidify the memory of the dream. It also has another purpose: if you can only journal later in the day, the key points you wrote earlier in the checklist can act as reminders, or "memory triggers," that will help you better recall your dream.

Many times dreams overtly alert us to longstanding patterns of behavior and belief (a.k.a. inner themes) that require our awareness in order for us to progress forward. *In other words, your dreams can act as a mirror helping you to see a reflection of your inner patterns by showing you repetitive dream scenarios, images, and symbols.* The checklist acts as an easy reference system you can review in order to recognize these themes!

All you need to do is to scan through multiple checklists (I recommend a minimum of ten) to see if any symbols, places, and dream figures repeat. If repetitive imagery does appear in your checklists, you know you are likely working with a theme. When you recognize a theme, note it in the "Themes" section of the associated checklist. Then work with the thematic information for your benefit.

You will also notice that I have placed a helpful section called "Feelings and Thoughts on All the Dream Themes Uncovered in This Journal" in the back of this book. This section has been created so that you can more easily reflect on *all of the themes* you uncover throughout this specific dream journal. The beauty of this is that if you then record your dream themes in multiple dream journals, it becomes very easy to review how your inner narrative changes over time.

Remember, a theme is any longstanding pattern of behavior, thought, or emotion that's made apparent through repetitive dream symbols, experiences, and images. For example, say you page through eleven checklists and find that you often dreamed of being chased or going into the same store. In this case, you would write down the themes of anxiety (being chased) and familiarity (the store) in the associated checklists.

In this dream example, you would also want to reflect on what the store was selling because it is likely linked to an inner theme you are identifying and addressing. You could ask yourself: *What does this particular store and its products represent for me?* For example, a clothing store could symbolically represent the themes of warmth or identity. Groceries could signify the need for sustenance and nurturance. A hardware store could be telling you that you need to build and repair something in your life or that you need new "emotional tools."

You may find that you discover both explicit and implicit dream themes through this self-reflective journaling process. You should record both kinds in the checklists. Explicit dream themes are generally quite obvious; they are the kinds of narratives you have over and over again (like having the same kind of anxiety-provoking nightmare or finding yourself in the same type of scenario night after night). Implicit dream themes, however, are discovered through reducing repetitive dream symbols into singular signs or meanings.

For example, cars, trains, and buses can all represent the theme of movement. The state of the transportation would also alert you to how well you were handling that form of movement. Say you have a number of dreams during which the common experience is a car breaking down. This dream imagery is helping you face any feelings of internal resistance you are experiencing in your waking life. In this case, you would mark the theme of "internal resistance" in the checklist so that you could work on resolving the issue you may be experiencing.

Once again, a theme can be anything that features prominently throughout multiple dream entries. As a further example, if you find that you are often chased or visit familiar childhood places in numerous dreams, those two experiences can be viewed as two consistent themes for you: anxiety and the past. Any repetitive emotion can individually encompass a theme, such as fear or love.

So if you find that you are dealing with consistent and repetitive dream themes, look to any patterns of learned behaviors (or even belief systems you may be experiencing) that need to be acknowledged, addressed, and altered in your life. Use your own intuitive and intellectual wisdom to help guide you in this process of self-discovery.

I'M READY TO CONNECT
WITH MY INNER IMAGE TO
SEE THE TRUTH OF MY DREAMS
AND DESIRES.

YOU ARE WHAT YOUR DEEPEST DESIRE IS.

AS IS YOUR DESIRE, SO IS YOUR INTENTION.

AS IS YOUR INTENTION, SO IS YOUR WILL.

AS IS YOUR WILL, SO IS YOUR DEED.

AS IS YOUR DEED, SO IS YOUR DESTINY.

——UPANISHADS

A DELIBERATE DREAMER SETS
STRONG INTENTIONS

Your dreams often point you in the direction of your most treasured intentions and desires, so it is only fitting to have space in this journal to write down your intentions! An intention is a wholehearted declaration of desire and will that you write down with the full optimism (and focused attention) that it will occur in the future. You will notice that after a number of dream entries, a curated section called Align and Intend, where you can write down your heartfelt intentions, is provided. May you call in and live your most beautifully aligned life.

SEED YOUR INTENTIONS.
WATER THEM WITH YOUR WORDS.
WATCH THEM BLOOM IN YOUR LIFE.

THE

Deliberate Dreamer's

JOURNAL

TURNING SLEEP INTO
A SACRED PRACTICE

We spend a third of our lives sleeping. In ancient wisdom traditions, this time was consciously cultivated in order to give the practitioner the best chance for experiencing healthy and restorative states of being—states all aimed toward greater well-being and spiritual enlightenment. You can begin to curate and cultivate your own sleep practice by bringing greater attention and mindfulness to the way you fall asleep.

We all know the experience: you fall asleep feeling stressed and then spend your dreams in a similar state of anxiety! So to dream well, you need to be able to sleep well. Here are some quick and helpful tips to get you started.

Caffeine and Cell Phone Free

A plethora of evidence-based studies show that drinking caffeine late in the day can negatively influence sleep. So the simple trick is to stop drinking caffeine by 2 pm. Equally, the blue light emitted from cell phones (and other screens) negatively impacts sleep because it tricks the body into thinking it is daylight. This in turn throws the body's circadian rhythm out of whack, which ultimately results in poor sleep. So in order to sleep well, these two simple things need to be mindfully managed.

Crisp Sheets

It's helpful to have a crisp and clean bed and bedroom to sleep in. The idea is that by cultivating a serene external environment, you begin to promote an internal sense of calm and serenity. And who doesn't love to get into a comfortable and inviting bed?

Consistency

Research has shown that going to bed at a similar time every night aids in enhancing sleep quality. Equally, the more consistent you become with your sleep and dream practice, the more valuable your dream experiences will become because you pay greater attention to them.

Clear Consciousness

Bring attention to how you fall asleep, and alter any pattern of behavior or thought that disturbs peaceful and receptive sleep. You can do this by practicing a mindfulness meditation such as the "Sound Asleep" meditation (which appears on page 5) after you lie down in bed. Relax your body, focus on your breath, and ease into a peaceful and calm state of being. If you find that you are ruminating, or if you feel very anxious, bring your attention back to the moment by slowly counting backward from 100. If you still find yourself awake, practice the meditation again. The more consistently you practice falling asleep mindfully, the easier it becomes to dream and sleep well.

Compassionate Intentions

Setting intentions before you sleep is helpful. You can say something like, "It is my intention to receive compassionate and helpful guidance on [the issue you are experiencing] in my dreams tonight. It will be easy for me to remember my dreams on waking."

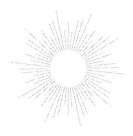

SOUND ASLEEP: A MEDITATION

Step 1: Begin by actively relaxing every part of your body.
Start at the tips of your toes, and end at the crown of your head. Simply focus on relaxing your body. Remember to release any tension held in your jaw and face muscles, too!

Step 2: Focus on your breath.
As you breathe in, think about experiencing restorative sleep and dreams. As you breathe out, let go of any tension you are feeling. Repeat this process at least nine times.

Step 3: Imagine feeling secure and at peace.
Picture your entire bedroom being covered in a beautiful green light. Imagine all the corners of your room—even your entire home—being washed with this emerald green light. Focus on feeling secure and at peace. Then extend this feeling outward. Do this for as long as you can. Imagine yourself sleeping safely, securely, and serenely.

Step 4: Set your dream intentions.

Always set the intention that you will easily remember your dreams upon waking. Then, if you have a particular issue or problem you would like guidance on, set your deliberate dream intentions at this point.

Step 5: Allow yourself to fall asleep.

Close your eyes, relax your body, and simply focus on mentally repeating your intentions until you fall asleep.

Download a free guided audio version of this meditation at athenalaz.com.

HOW TO RECALL
YOUR DREAMS

When you wake up, you'll have a fleeting moment when your dreams are still crystal clear. The trick to being able to recall your dreams is to actively use that brief time well. You can do this by remaining absolutely physically still the moment you wake up. Remaining physically still while you replay a dream over in your mind helps lock the dream in your memory. Then, when you are ready, grab this journal and write down the key dream points in the checklist and blank journal pages.

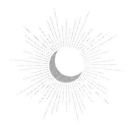

THE SPECTRUM OF YOUR DREAMS

H ave you ever experienced déjà vu? You know, a flash in time when you get the distinct sensation you've already witnessed or experienced that very moment. Déjà vu happens without warning and often when you least expect it. Generally you feel excited and bewildered when it happens because it throws you out of your usual automatic thinking and pulls you into the very present moment.

We are invited to become more aware through a déjà vu experience. In fact, the phrase itself means "already seen," so it makes sense that during the moment you might say to yourself, "Aha! There is a familiarity to this. What does that mean? Is there something I should be learning here? Is my mind simply catching up with itself? Or is universal wisdom beckoning me to do something different, maybe even better, this time around?"

Déjà rêvé is another wonderful French phrase, which means "already dreamed." It's when you recognize that you have already dreamed the very experience you are living through. The difference between déjà vu and déjà rêvé is that the repetition of the memory is experienced slightly differently.

Déjà vu is experienced as "I've lived this before"; déjà rêvé is "I've dreamed this before, *and now I'm living it.*" Both experiences have been documented throughout history, with the philosopher Pythagoras even describing déjà vu some 2,000 years ago. Currently neuroscientists are researching the entire spectrum of déjà experiences—to date, 20 differentiations have been defined—to discover the associated brain functioning that occurs when they happen.

I love that we get to experience déjà rêvé, and as someone who works with dreams, I believe it happens more often than people may realize. Sadly, many people fail to remember their dreams, so they miss out on the incredible experiences associated with dreaming—like déjà rêvé!

But here you are, dear dreamer, on the precipice of your inner world, and by keeping this journal, you will leap into the depths of it. With every word you write, you turn more of your attention toward your dreams and your intrapsychic life strengthens.

In psychological terms, you could say that through dream journaling, you are tending to your instinctual nature. That is, you are strengthening the dynamic between your mind and your inner world by declaring a robust intention to recall your dreams, recording them daily, and taking positive action. As a result, you may notice that your life begins to flourish, you dream more vividly, and the nightly guidance you receive becomes even more helpful!

The longer you consistently journal, the more likely you are to become aware of the magnificent connection between your waking life and your dream life—as well as the metaconsciousness that affords you the opportunity to experience both states of being. Wild stuff!

Ultimately, all dreams are helpful, even if they have an intense quality to them. In the following sections I've listed and clarified some of the different types of dreams. You will also notice that there is a space in every checklist to write down what kind of dreams you experience. On later reflection, you may be surprised to notice that you often dream in a series or that you've had more precognitive dreams than you originally thought! It is, after all, your dream adventure, with you as the key dreamer.

Symbolic Dreams

A symbol is something that illustrates more than what is obvious. Your dreams are filled with guidance and meaning imbued within symbolic images that you experience nightly. For example, say you dream of an ice-cream truck running over your favorite handbag (if you don't own a handbag, just go with this) while you watch in disappointment. Upon waking, you would interpret the dream based on three symbols: the ice-cream truck, the action of the truck, and the handbag.

Ice-cream trucks as symbolic images can evoke nostalgic memories of a time past, childhood fondness, and carefree ease. Yet in the dream, the ice-cream truck runs over your best bag. Ugh!

The dream comes to show you that your childhood nostalgia is impeding something you "favor" in your waking life. You know this because the truck of your childhood past runs over your favorite bag. The dream may be symbolically telling you that you are putting too much attention on your past and not focusing enough on where you find yourself right now. In other words, your current emotional joy is being overrun by indulging in thoughts of what was. Ultimately, symbolic dreams are wonderful, and you will find that the more you work with them, the easier it becomes to decipher their meanings.

Lucid Dreams

Lucid dreams are incredible—so much so that Tibetan *Bön* Buddhists assign dream and sleep yoga (of which lucid dreaming is a part) as a pathway to enlightenment. Simply put, lucid dreams are dreams in which you are actively aware that you are dreaming *while you are actually in the dream*. Lucid dreaming is an ancient dream practice that affords the dreamer (you) the opportunity to transcend any limiting beliefs by working with the dreamscape *directly and consciously.* This ancient art of dreaming has been practiced worldwide and is in a current resurgence in the collective consciousness. If you'd like to learn how to lucid dream and discover all the benefits that come with it, see my book *The Alchemy of Your Dreams: A Modern Guide to the Ancient Art of Lucid Dreaming and Interpretation.*

Announcing Dreams

From the Pacific Northwest to the shores of Korea, announcing dreams have been documented across the world. In essence, a pregnant woman receives a dream that announces important information about the baby she is carrying! Different cultures assign different meanings to the dream information: it can be about the reincarnation cycle, the sex of the baby, or more personally focused familial information.

Interestingly enough, many research studies have shown that the sex of the baby is often correctly correlated to the dream information. In one study, 26 of 29 mothers had announcing dreams identifying their baby's gender that later turned out to be accurate.

Some theorists argue that it is the mother's own subconscious (the unknown depths of the mind) that makes these dreams occur. Others believe the baby's spirit gifts the mother the dream. No matter how these dreams come to be, announcing dreams are incredible, and many people know to pay attention to them. Currently, researchers across the world are attempting to discover more about these dreams by studying them in greater depth.

Series Dreams

Ever watched a miniseries? Well, that's what these kinds of dreams are like! Swiss psychiatrist Carl Jung first noted these types of dreams when he recognized that his patients would dream in a series-like manner. In essence, the psyche picks up where it last left off by continuing with the same dream story line or narrative over a period of time. These types of dreams hold emotional and psychological weight because they usually occur when you are on the brink of some sort of significant breakthrough. Generally, because these types of dreams can be complex in meaning and easy to misunderstand, dream analysts often help decipher and work with them. If you find that you are dreaming in a series, it may be well worth your while to take your dream content (or journal!) to a dream guide who can help you see the larger picture.

Warning Dreams

There is no way to spin a warning dream other than to tell you that the positive thing to do is to really pay attention to this type of dream. Warning dreams are exactly that: they warn you of something you are not currently aware of but should be. These kinds of dreams tend to be vivid and very in your face, so much so that they are very hard to dismiss in the morning—which ultimately is the whole point! The warning could be about a relationship dynamic, your loved ones, a problem you are unaware of, or even a health issue. Warning dreams are often highly personal and, if acted on in a positive manner, can be incredibly helpful. You will recognize a warning dream because you won't be able to shake the feeling that your dream was different than usual and significant. The old adage "better safe than sorry" really applies here!

Repetitive Dreams

Repetitive dreams are often confused with dreams in a series but they are not the same. A repetitive dream is a dream that you have over and over again. The dream imagery is almost identical each time, and you find yourself replaying the same situation, or repeating the same action, night after night. A series dream, on the other hand, picks up from the point you left off in the previous dream. The dream itself follows a much larger narrative than a repetitive dream, which repeats the same imagery.

Repetitive dreams help resolve and transform memories, emotions, or scenarios that are difficult to face in life. They help you summon your inner courage to look at what pains or frightens you so that you can release the burden. Generally, people tend to have repetitive dreams in which they are being hunted down, chased, or trapped in small spaces. The imagery is helpful in alerting you to the pattern that is making you feel scared, anxious, and stuck.

Nightmares

From pandemic dreams to menacing figures, these dreams need no introduction. There are many theories as to why we have nightmares. Some researchers argue that nightmares act as an evolutionary function that primes us for greater safety and survival. Depth psychologists maintain there is so much more to nightmares than just evolutionary functioning, including emotional processing, facing repressed fears, and surpassing upper limits. As humans, we are both our biology and our beliefs, so I believe that both schools of thought have validity. Ultimately, no one enjoys a nightmare, but you still can benefit from the information found within these dreams. You can work with a nightmare through journaling or by incubating a lucid dream (that is when you interact and change the nightmare within the actual dream).

Precognitive Dreams

Prophetic or precognitive dreams have been recorded for centuries. Shrouded in mystery and awe, these dreams have the power to alert the dreamer to the state of well-being of the collective or to more private but equally important information. Many people worldwide have recorded and shared dreams that alerted them to disasters before they happened. For example, there are many different accounts of people dreaming of cars being washed away just before the catastrophic tsunami hit Japan in 2011. Precognitive dreams remind us that we are all connected and that the well-being of the planet is woven through the actions we all take. Reverence and precognitive dreaming go hand in hand.

Healing Dreams

I believe the foundation of all dreams is built on an intention of healing. I know that may sound a bit strange, but every dream, in some form or another, is telling you something, *is guiding you*. So if you use that guidance well, you will see an active difference in your life. Isn't that comforting to know?

Healing dreams as a specific type of dream are those in which you feel like you've transmuted or overcome something in the actual dream. For example, many people have dreamed of late family members with whom they had some difficulty in life only to "forgive" one another in the dreamscape. Ultimately, healing dreams are highly subjective yet wondrously helpful at the same time. They tend to point dreamers back to wholeness and well-being.

THE DELIBERATE DREAMER'S
JOURNEY

My Dream Experiences

My dreams point me in the direction of my destiny.

....

....

....

....

....

....

....

....

....

....

....

....

....

....

WHAT ACTION AM I BEING GUIDED TO TAKE?

What kind of dream was this?

SYMBOLIC ○ LUCID ○ ANNOUNCING ○ SERIES ○ WARNING ○

REPETITIVE ○ NIGHTMARE ○ PRECOGNITIVE ○ HEALING ○

How did my dream make me feel?

....

Prominent symbols

....

....

....

....

....

Places in my dream

....

....

....

....

People in my dream

....

....

....

....

Themes

....

....

....

....

My Dream Experiences

My dreams are soul-speak, gently guiding me toward my inner light.

WHAT ACTION AM I BEING GUIDED TO TAKE?

....

....

....

....

....

....

....

....

....

....

....

....

....

....

What kind of dream was this?

SYMBOLIC ◯ LUCID ◯ ANNOUNCING ◯ SERIES ◯ WARNING ◯

REPETITIVE ◯ NIGHTMARE ◯ PRECOGNITIVE ◯ HEALING ◯

How did my dream make me feel?

....

Prominent symbols

....

....

....

....

Places in my dream

....

....

....

....

People in my dream

....

....

....

....

Themes

....

....

....

....

My Dream Experiences

There are no mistakes in the dream symbols I see.
They are specific, purposeful, and right on time.

....

....

....

....

....

....

....

....

....

....

....

....

....

WHAT ACTION AM I BEING GUIDED TO TAKE?

What kind of dream was this?

SYMBOLIC ○ LUCID ○ ANNOUNCING ○ SERIES ○ WARNING ○

REPETITIVE ○ NIGHTMARE ○ PRECOGNITIVE ○ HEALING ○

How did my dream make me feel?

....

Prominent symbols

....

....

....

....

....

Places in my dream

....

....

....

....

People in my dream

....

....

....

....

Themes

....

....

....

....

My Dream Experiences

My dreams guide me forward positively.

....

....

....

....

....

....

....

....

....

....

....

....

WHAT ACTION AM I BEING GUIDED TO TAKE?

What kind of dream was this?

SYMBOLIC ○ LUCID ○ ANNOUNCING ○ SERIES ○ WARNING ○

REPETITIVE ○ NIGHTMARE ○ PRECOGNITIVE ○ HEALING ○

How did my dream make me feel?

....

Prominent symbols

....

....

....

....

Places in my dream

....

....

....

....

People in my dream

....

....

....

....

Themes

....

....

....

....

My Dream Experiences

I connect with my true nature every night.

....

....

....

....

....

....

....

....

....

....

....

....

....

....

....

....

WHAT ACTION AM I BEING GUIDED TO TAKE?

What kind of dream was this?

SYMBOLIC ○ LUCID ○ ANNOUNCING ○ SERIES ○ WARNING ○

REPETITIVE ○ NIGHTMARE ○ PRECOGNITIVE ○ HEALING ○

How did my dream make me feel?

....

Prominent symbols

....

....

....

....

....

Places in my dream

....

....

....

....

....

People in my dream

....

....

....

....

....

Themes

....

....

....

....

....

My Dream Experiences

I access universal guidance and wisdom when I dream.

....

....

....

....

....

....

....

....

....

....

....

....

....

....

WHAT ACTION AM I BEING GUIDED TO TAKE?

What kind of dream was this?

SYMBOLIC ○ **LUCID** ○ **ANNOUNCING** ○ **SERIES** ○ **WARNING** ○

REPETITIVE ○ **NIGHTMARE** ○ **PRECOGNITIVE** ○ **HEALING** ○

How did my dream make me feel?

....

Prominent symbols

....

....

....

....

....

Places in my dream

....

....

....

....

People in my dream

....

....

....

....

Themes

....

....

....

....

My Dream Experiences

Why this dream, in this way, right now?

WHAT ACTION AM I BEING GUIDED TO TAKE?

What kind of dream was this?

SYMBOLIC ◯ LUCID ◯ ANNOUNCING ◯ SERIES ◯ WARNING ◯

REPETITIVE ◯ NIGHTMARE ◯ PRECOGNITIVE ◯ HEALING ◯

How did my dream make me feel?

....

Prominent symbols

....

....

....

....

....

Places in my dream

....

....

....

....

People in my dream

....

....

....

....

Themes

....

....

....

....

ALIGN AND INTEND

Set your intentions in the space below.

I am ready to
receive what
I have been
asking for.

RELEASE TO RECEIVE

What do I need to let go of in order to see
my intentions come to life?

....

....

....

....

....

....

....

....

....   I am ready to

....   move beyond

....   the confines

....   of my past to

....   welcome in

....   my brilliant

....   future.

THE DELIBERATE DREAMER'S

JOURNEY

My Dream Experiences

Tonight I will experience incredible dreams of clarity, and
I will be able to recall my experiences upon waking.

....

....

....

....

....

....

....

....

....

....

....

....

WHAT ACTION AM I BEING GUIDED TO TAKE?

What kind of dream was this?

SYMBOLIC ○ LUCID ○ ANNOUNCING ○ SERIES ○ WARNING ○

REPETITIVE ○ NIGHTMARE ○ PRECOGNITIVE ○ HEALING ○

How did my dream make me feel?

....

Prominent symbols

....

....

....

....

....

Places in my dream

....

....

....

....

People in my dream

....

....

....

....

Themes

....

....

....

....

My Dream Experiences

May my dreams help me remember my deepest strengths so I can face any problem with serenity, ease, and fortitude in the light of day.

....

....

....

....

....

....

....

....

....

....

....

....

WHAT ACTION AM I BEING GUIDED TO TAKE?

What kind of dream was this?

SYMBOLIC ○ LUCID ○ ANNOUNCING ○ SERIES ○ WARNING ○

REPETITIVE ○ NIGHTMARE ○ PRECOGNITIVE ○ HEALING ○

How did my dream make me feel?

....

Prominent symbols

....

....

....

....

Places in my dream

....

....

....

....

People in my dream

....

....

....

....

Themes

....

....

....

....

My Dream Experiences

In the infinity of my dreams, I discover that I am always guided.

....

....

....

....

....

....

....

....

....

....

....

....

....

....

....

....

....

....

....

....

....

WHAT ACTION AM I BEING GUIDED TO TAKE?

What kind of dream was this?

SYMBOLIC ◯ LUCID ◯ ANNOUNCING ◯ SERIES ◯ WARNING ◯

REPETITIVE ◯ NIGHTMARE ◯ PRECOGNITIVE ◯ HEALING ◯

How did my dream make me feel?

....

Prominent symbols

....

....

....

....

....

Places in my dream

....

....

....

....

....

People in my dream

....

....

....

....

....

Themes

....

....

....

....

....

My Dream Experiences

I call on deep peace to reside in my body, heart, and mind.

....

....

....

....

....

....

....

....

....

....

....

....

....

WHAT ACTION AM I BEING GUIDED TO TAKE?

What kind of dream was this?

SYMBOLIC ◯ LUCID ◯ ANNOUNCING ◯ SERIES ◯ WARNING ◯
REPETITIVE ◯ NIGHTMARE ◯ PRECOGNITIVE ◯ HEALING ◯

How did my dream make me feel?

....

Prominent symbols

....

....

....

....

....

Places in my dream

....

....

....

....

People in my dream

....

....

....

....

Themes

....

....

....

....

My Dream Experiences

I am calm in the face of uncertainty.

....

....

....

....

....

....

....

....

....

....

....

....

....

....

WHAT ACTION AM I BEING GUIDED TO TAKE?

What kind of dream was this?

SYMBOLIC ○ LUCID ○ ANNOUNCING ○ SERIES ○ WARNING ○

REPETITIVE ○ NIGHTMARE ○ PRECOGNITIVE ○ HEALING ○

How did my dream make me feel?

....

Prominent symbols

....

....

....

....

....

Places in my dream

....

....

....

....

....

People in my dream

....

....

....

....

Themes

....

....

....

....

My Dream Experiences

My dreams always provide me with helpful solutions and guidance.

....

....

....

....

....

....

....

....

....

....

....

....

....

WHAT ACTION AM I BEING GUIDED TO TAKE?

What kind of dream was this?

SYMBOLIC ○ **LUCID** ○ **ANNOUNCING** ○ **SERIES** ○ **WARNING** ○
REPETITIVE ○ **NIGHTMARE** ○ **PRECOGNITIVE** ○ **HEALING** ○

How did my dream make me feel?

....

Prominent symbols

....

....

....

....

....

Places in my dream

....

....

....

....

People in my dream

....

....

....

....

Themes

....

....

....

....

My Dream Experiences

At all times, I am guided, safe, and secure.

WHAT ACTION AM I BEING GUIDED TO TAKE?

What kind of dream was this?

SYMBOLIC ◯ LUCID ◯ ANNOUNCING ◯ SERIES ◯ WARNING ◯

REPETITIVE ◯ NIGHTMARE ◯ PRECOGNITIVE ◯ HEALING ◯

How did my dream make me feel?

....

Prominent symbols

....

....

....

....

....

Places in my dream

....

....

....

....

....

People in my dream

....

....

....

....

Themes

....

....

....

....

ALIGN AND INTEND

Set your intentions in the space below.

_____

_____

_____

_____

_____

_____

_____

_____

I am
constantly
creating a life
filled with
love, joy, and
meaning.

RELEASE TO RECEIVE

What do I need to let go of in order to see
my intentions come to life?

I am ready to
move beyond
the confines
of my past to
welcome in my
brilliant future.

THE DELIBERATE DREAMER'S

JOURNEY

My Dream Experiences

My dreams always provide me with creative
possibilities and solutions.

....

....

....

....

....

....

....

....

....

....

....

....

....

....

....

....

WHAT ACTION AM I BEING GUIDED TO TAKE?

What kind of dream was this?

SYMBOLIC ○ LUCID ○ ANNOUNCING ○ SERIES ○ WARNING ○

REPETITIVE ○ NIGHTMARE ○ PRECOGNITIVE ○ HEALING ○

How did my dream make me feel?

....

Prominent symbols

....

....

....

....

....

Places in my dream

....

....

....

....

People in my dream

....

....

....

....

Themes

....

....

....

....

My Dream Experiences

Love, serenity, and ease are always available to me when I look within.

....

....

....

....

....

....

....

....

....

....

....

....

....

....

....

WHAT ACTION AM I BEING GUIDED TO TAKE?

What kind of dream was this?

SYMBOLIC ○ LUCID ○ ANNOUNCING ○ SERIES ○ WARNING ○

REPETITIVE ○ NIGHTMARE ○ PRECOGNITIVE ○ HEALING ○

How did my dream make me feel?

....

Prominent symbols

....

....

....

....

....

Places in my dream

....

....

....

....

People in my dream

....

....

....

....

Themes

....

....

....

....

My Dream Experiences

I speak well of my future, and so it is.

....

....

....

....

....

....

....

....

....

....

....

....

....

WHAT ACTION AM I BEING GUIDED TO TAKE?

What kind of dream was this?

SYMBOLIC ○ LUCID ○ ANNOUNCING ○ SERIES ○ WARNING ○

REPETITIVE ○ NIGHTMARE ○ PRECOGNITIVE ○ HEALING ○

How did my dream make me feel?

....

Prominent symbols

....

....

....

....

....

Places in my dream

....

....

....

....

....

People in my dream

....

....

....

....

....

Themes

....

....

....

....

....

My Dream Experiences

My heart is open, and I allow myself to feel fully.

....

....

....

....

....

....

....

....

....

....

....

....

....

....

WHAT ACTION AM I BEING GUIDED TO TAKE?

What kind of dream was this?

SYMBOLIC ○ LUCID ○ ANNOUNCING ○ SERIES ○ WARNING ○

REPETITIVE ○ NIGHTMARE ○ PRECOGNITIVE ○ HEALING ○

How did my dream make me feel?

....

Prominent symbols

....

....

....

....

....

Places in my dream

....

....

....

....

People in my dream

....

....

....

....

Themes

....

....

....

....

My Dream Experiences

Everything is happening in perfect order.

....

....

....

....

....

....

....

....

....

....

....

....

WHAT ACTION AM I BEING GUIDED TO TAKE?

What kind of dream was this?

SYMBOLIC ◯ LUCID ◯ ANNOUNCING ◯ SERIES ◯ WARNING ◯

REPETITIVE ◯ NIGHTMARE ◯ PRECOGNITIVE ◯ HEALING ◯

How did my dream make me feel?

....

Prominent symbols

....

....

....

....

....

Places in my dream

....

....

....

....

People in my dream

....

....

....

....

Themes

....

....

....

....

My Dream Experiences

DATE: _____

I am in harmony with my life and dreams.

....

....

....

....

....

....

....

....

....

....

....

....

WHAT ACTION AM I BEING GUIDED TO TAKE?

What kind of dream was this?

SYMBOLIC ○ LUCID ○ ANNOUNCING ○ SERIES ○ WARNING ○

REPETITIVE ○ NIGHTMARE ○ PRECOGNITIVE ○ HEALING ○

How did my dream make me feel?

....

Prominent symbols

....

....

....

....

....

Places in my dream

....

....

....

....

People in my dream

....

....

....

....

Themes

....

....

....

....

My Dream Experiences

My psyche finds balance through the medium of my dreams.

....

....

....

....

....

....

....

....

....

....

....

....

WHAT ACTION AM I BEING GUIDED TO TAKE?

What kind of dream was this?

SYMBOLIC ○ LUCID ○ ANNOUNCING ○ SERIES ○ WARNING ○

REPETITIVE ○ NIGHTMARE ○ PRECOGNITIVE ○ HEALING ○

How did my dream make me feel?

....

Prominent symbols

....

....

....

....

....

Places in my dream

....

....

....

....

....

People in my dream

....

....

....

....

....

Themes

....

....

....

....

....

ALIGN AND INTEND

Set your intentions in the space below.

_____

_____

_____

_____

_____

_____

_____

_____

I am willing
to step into
the mystery of
the unknown
to embrace a
life beyond
my wildest
dreams.

RELEASE TO RECEIVE

What do I need to let go of to see my intentions come to life?

....

....

....

....

....

....

....

....

....   I am ready to
                                                                           move beyond
....   the confines
                                                                           of my past to
....   welcome in
                                                                           my brilliant
....   future.

THE DELIBERATE DREAMER'S

JOURNEY

My Dream Experiences

I am ready to experience BIG dreams!

....

....

....

....

....

....

....

....

....

....

....

....

WHAT ACTION AM I BEING GUIDED TO TAKE?

What kind of dream was this?

SYMBOLIC ○ LUCID ○ ANNOUNCING ○ SERIES ○ WARNING ○

REPETITIVE ○ NIGHTMARE ○ PRECOGNITIVE ○ HEALING ○

How did my dream make me feel?

....

Prominent symbols

....

....

....

....

....

Places in my dream

....

....

....

....

....

People in my dream

....

....

....

....

Themes

....

....

....

....

My Dream Experiences

I afford myself the time I need to heal.

WHAT ACTION AM I BEING GUIDED TO TAKE?

What kind of dream was this?

SYMBOLIC ○ LUCID ○ ANNOUNCING ○ SERIES ○ WARNING ○

REPETITIVE ○ NIGHTMARE ○ PRECOGNITIVE ○ HEALING ○

How did my dream make me feel?

....

Prominent symbols

....

....

....

....

....

Places in my dream

....

....

....

....

....

People in my dream

....

....

....

....

Themes

....

....

....

....

My Dream Experiences

My dreams show me the best path forward.

WHAT ACTION AM I BEING GUIDED TO TAKE?

What kind of dream was this?

SYMBOLIC ○ LUCID ○ ANNOUNCING ○ SERIES ○ WARNING ○

REPETITIVE ○ NIGHTMARE ○ PRECOGNITIVE ○ HEALING ○

How did my dream make me feel?

....

Prominent symbols

....

....

....

....

....

Places in my dream

....

....

....

....

People in my dream

....

....

....

....

Themes

....

....

....

....

My Dream Experiences

Every person I meet in my dreams is showing me something valuable.

WHAT ACTION AM I BEING GUIDED TO TAKE?

What kind of dream was this?

SYMBOLIC ○ LUCID ○ ANNOUNCING ○ SERIES ○ WARNING ○

REPETITIVE ○ NIGHTMARE ○ PRECOGNITIVE ○ HEALING ○

How did my dream make me feel?

....

Prominent symbols

....

....

....

....

....

Places in my dream

....

....

....

....

....

People in my dream

....

....

....

....

Themes

....

....

....

....

My Dream Experiences

My inner vision is clear.

....

....

....

....

....

....

....

....

....

....

....

WHAT ACTION AM I BEING GUIDED TO TAKE?

What kind of dream was this?

SYMBOLIC ○ LUCID ○ ANNOUNCING ○ SERIES ○ WARNING ○

REPETITIVE ○ NIGHTMARE ○ PRECOGNITIVE ○ HEALING ○

How did my dream make me feel?

....

Prominent symbols

....

....

....

....

....

Places in my dream

....

....

....

....

People in my dream

....

....

....

....

Themes

....

....

....

....

My Dream Experiences

DATE: _____

I trust the timing of my dreams.

....

....

....

....

....

....

....

....

....

....

....

....

....

....

WHAT ACTION AM I BEING GUIDED TO TAKE?

What kind of dream was this?

SYMBOLIC ○ LUCID ○ ANNOUNCING ○ SERIES ○ WARNING ○

REPETITIVE ○ NIGHTMARE ○ PRECOGNITIVE ○ HEALING ○

How did my dream make me feel?

....

Prominent symbols

....

....

....

....

Places in my dream

....

....

....

....

People in my dream

....

....

....

....

Themes

....

....

....

....

My Dream Experiences

DATE: _____

Everything I need to know, I discover in my dreams.

....

....

....

....

....

....

....

....

....

....

....

....

WHAT ACTION AM I BEING GUIDED TO TAKE?

What kind of dream was this?

SYMBOLIC ○ LUCID ○ ANNOUNCING ○ SERIES ○ WARNING ○

REPETITIVE ○ NIGHTMARE ○ PRECOGNITIVE ○ HEALING ○

How did my dream make me feel?

....

Prominent symbols

....

....

....

....

....

Places in my dream

....

....

....

....

People in my dream

....

....

....

....

Themes

....

....

....

....

ALIGN AND INTEND

Set your intentions in the space below.

....

....

....

....

....

....

....

....

....

....

I cultivate
how I want
to feel with
my attention
and mindful
awareness.

RELEASE TO RECEIVE

What do I need to let go of to see my intentions come to life?

....

....

....

....

....

....

....

....

....

I am ready to
....

move beyond
....

the confines
....

of my past to
....

welcome in
....

my brilliant
....

future.

THE DELIBERATE DREAMER'S

JOURNEY

My Dream Experiences

I am in harmony with all that is.

....

....

....

....

....

....

....

....

....

....

....

....

....

WHAT ACTION AM I BEING GUIDED TO TAKE?

What kind of dream was this?

SYMBOLIC ○ LUCID ○ ANNOUNCING ○ SERIES ○ WARNING ○

REPETITIVE ○ NIGHTMARE ○ PRECOGNITIVE ○ HEALING ○

How did my dream make me feel?

....

Prominent symbols

....

....

....

....

Places in my dream

....

....

....

....

People in my dream

....

....

....

....

Themes

....

....

....

....

My Dream Experiences

When I fall into doubt, I breathe and let go.

....

....

....

....

....

....

....

....

....

....

....

....

WHAT ACTION AM I BEING GUIDED TO TAKE?

What kind of dream was this?

SYMBOLIC ○ LUCID ○ ANNOUNCING ○ SERIES ○ WARNING ○

REPETITIVE ○ NIGHTMARE ○ PRECOGNITIVE ○ HEALING ○

How did my dream make me feel?

....

Prominent symbols

....

....

....

....

Places in my dream

....

....

....

....

People in my dream

....

....

....

....

Themes

....

....

....

....

My Dream Experiences

I easily release what is not working for me.

WHAT ACTION AM I BEING GUIDED TO TAKE?

What kind of dream was this?

SYMBOLIC ○ LUCID ○ ANNOUNCING ○ SERIES ○ WARNING ○

REPETITIVE ○ NIGHTMARE ○ PRECOGNITIVE ○ HEALING ○

How did my dream make me feel?

....

Prominent symbols

....

....

....

....

....

Places in my dream

....

....

....

....

People in my dream

....

....

....

....

Themes

....

....

....

....

My Dream Experiences

My inner images are rich in insight and meaning.
I easily tap into my inner guidance system.

....

....

....

....

....

....

....

....

....

....

....

....

WHAT ACTION AM I BEING GUIDED TO TAKE?

What kind of dream was this?

SYMBOLIC ○ LUCID ○ ANNOUNCING ○ SERIES ○ WARNING ○

REPETITIVE ○ NIGHTMARE ○ PRECOGNITIVE ○ HEALING ○

How did my dream make me feel?

....

Prominent symbols

....

....

....

....

....

Places in my dream

....

....

....

....

....

People in my dream

....

....

....

....

Themes

....

....

....

....

My Dream Experiences

Good things are on the way.

....

....

....

....

....

....

....

....

....

....

....

....

....

WHAT ACTION AM I BEING GUIDED TO TAKE?

What kind of dream was this?

SYMBOLIC ○ LUCID ○ ANNOUNCING ○ SERIES ○ WARNING ○

REPETITIVE ○ NIGHTMARE ○ PRECOGNITIVE ○ HEALING ○

How did my dream make me feel?

....

Prominent symbols

....

....

....

....

....

Places in my dream

....

....

....

....

People in my dream

....

....

....

....

Themes

....

....

....

....

My Dream Experiences

What is meant for me is on its way to me.

....

....

....

....

....

....

....

....

....

....

....

....

WHAT ACTION AM I BEING GUIDED TO TAKE?

What kind of dream was this?

SYMBOLIC ○ LUCID ○ ANNOUNCING ○ SERIES ○ WARNING ○

REPETITIVE ○ NIGHTMARE ○ PRECOGNITIVE ○ HEALING ○

How did my dream make me feel?

....

Prominent symbols

....

....

....

....

....

Places in my dream

....

....

....

....

....

People in my dream

....

....

....

....

Themes

....

....

....

....

My Dream Experiences

I trust in my ability to respond well to any situation that arises.

....

....

....

....

....

....

....

....

....

....

....

....

....

WHAT ACTION AM I BEING GUIDED TO TAKE?

What kind of dream was this?

SYMBOLIC ○ LUCID ○ ANNOUNCING ○ SERIES ○ WARNING ○

REPETITIVE ○ NIGHTMARE ○ PRECOGNITIVE ○ HEALING ○

How did my dream make me feel?

....

Prominent symbols

....

....

....

....

....

Places in my dream

....

....

....

....

....

People in my dream

....

....

....

....

....

Themes

....

....

....

....

....

ALIGN AND INTEND

Set your intentions in the space below.

....

....

....

....

....

....

....

....

....

I have the
power to
create the
reality I wish
to see.

....

....

....

....

RELEASE TO RECEIVE

What do I need to let go of to see my
intentions come to life?

I am ready to
move beyond
the confines
of my past to
welcome in
my brilliant
future.

THE DELIBERATE DREAMER'S
JOURNEY

My Dream Experiences

My dreams guide me back home.

....

....

....

....

....

....

....

....

....

....

....

....

WHAT ACTION AM I BEING GUIDED TO TAKE?

What kind of dream was this?

SYMBOLIC ◯ LUCID ◯ ANNOUNCING ◯ SERIES ◯ WARNING ◯

REPETITIVE ◯ NIGHTMARE ◯ PRECOGNITIVE ◯ HEALING ◯

How did my dream make me feel?

....

Prominent symbols

....

....

....

....

....

Places in my dream

....

....

....

....

....

People in my dream

....

....

....

....

Themes

....

....

....

....

My Dream Experiences

My perception is a result of learning, and I can change it at any time.

WHAT ACTION AM I BEING GUIDED TO TAKE?

What kind of dream was this?

SYMBOLIC ○ LUCID ○ ANNOUNCING ○ SERIES ○ WARNING ○

REPETITIVE ○ NIGHTMARE ○ PRECOGNITIVE ○ HEALING ○

How did my dream make me feel?

....

Prominent symbols

....

....

....

....

....

Places in my dream

....

....

....

....

People in my dream

....

....

....

....

Themes

....

....

....

....

My Dream Experiences

In this moment, I invite more love into my life.

....

....

....

....

....

....

....

....

....

....

....

....

WHAT ACTION AM I BEING GUIDED TO TAKE?

What kind of dream was this?

SYMBOLIC ○ LUCID ○ ANNOUNCING ○ SERIES ○ WARNING ○

REPETITIVE ○ NIGHTMARE ○ PRECOGNITIVE ○ HEALING ○

How did my dream make me feel?

....

Prominent symbols

....

....

....

....

....

Places in my dream

....

....

....

....

....

People in my dream

....

....

....

....

Themes

....

....

....

....

My Dream Experiences

My dreams always help me lead with my heart.

....

....

....

....

....

....

....

....

....

....

....

....

....

....

....

....

....

....

WHAT ACTION AM I BEING GUIDED TO TAKE?

What kind of dream was this?

SYMBOLIC ○ LUCID ○ ANNOUNCING ○ SERIES ○ WARNING ○

REPETITIVE ○ NIGHTMARE ○ PRECOGNITIVE ○ HEALING ○

How did my dream make me feel?

....

Prominent symbols

....

....

....

....

....

Places in my dream

....

....

....

....

....

People in my dream

....

....

....

....

....

Themes

....

....

....

....

....

My Dream Experiences

I am supported and guided by the mystery that weaves dreams.

....

....

....

....

....

....

....

....

....

....

....

....

....

WHAT ACTION AM I BEING GUIDED TO TAKE?

What kind of dream was this?

SYMBOLIC ◯ LUCID ◯ ANNOUNCING ◯ SERIES ◯ WARNING ◯

REPETITIVE ◯ NIGHTMARE ◯ PRECOGNITIVE ◯ HEALING ◯

How did my dream make me feel?

....

Prominent symbols

....

....

....

....

....

Places in my dream

....

....

....

....

People in my dream

....

....

....

....

Themes

....

....

....

....

My Dream Experiences

I am a dream-teller, speaking life to my visions.

....

....

....

....

....

....

....

....

....

....

....

....

....

WHAT ACTION AM I BEING GUIDED TO TAKE?

What kind of dream was this?

SYMBOLIC ○ LUCID ○ ANNOUNCING ○ SERIES ○ WARNING ○

REPETITIVE ○ NIGHTMARE ○ PRECOGNITIVE ○ HEALING ○

How did my dream make me feel?

....

Prominent symbols

....

....

....

....

Places in my dream

....

....

....

....

People in my dream

....

....

....

....

Themes

....

....

....

....

My Dream Experiences

I am always connected to the greater consciousness
behind my dream images.

....

....

....

....

....

....

....

....

....

....

....

....

....

WHAT ACTION AM I BEING GUIDED TO TAKE?

What kind of dream was this?

SYMBOLIC ○ LUCID ○ ANNOUNCING ○ SERIES ○ WARNING ○

REPETITIVE ○ NIGHTMARE ○ PRECOGNITIVE ○ HEALING ○

How did my dream make me feel?

....

Prominent symbols

....

....

....

....

....

Places in my dream

....

....

....

....

People in my dream

....

....

....

....

Themes

....

....

....

....

ALIGN AND INTEND

Set your intentions in the space below.

....

....

....

....

....

....

....

....

I easily
connect to
my intuition
and I use the
guidance I
receive to
take positive
action.

....

....

....

....

....

....

....

RELEASE TO RECEIVE

What do I need to let go of to see my intentions come to life?

....

....

....

....

....

....

....

....

....   I am ready to
....   move beyond
....   the confines
....   of my past to
....   welcome in
....   my brilliant
....   future.

10 COMMON DREAM THEMES AND THEIR UNIVERSAL MEANINGS

NATURE

Nature symbols speak to something intrinsic within you: a primal force that can either nurture life or destroy it. When you dream of symbols related to nature, you are being invited to look at the wilderness within—your personality traits, instincts, and behaviors and how they impact your life.

Nature is also representative of creation in all its manifestations and forms. So your dreams may mimic nature's cycles to show you how to better handle the "season" you are in. In other words, your dreams will offer a solution on how to best cope with the current transition or period of change you are in. If you find yourself gardening in a dream, you may need to prune away a relationship or pattern in your life. Or the dream may be telling you to actively sow fruitful seeds for your future.

Nature dream symbols also speak to your relationship and connection with the earth itself. Are you respectful and protective of it? The earth is a living entity that provides all the food, water, and air we need to survive and without which we would cease to exist. And so nature dreams can highlight the state of our personal well-being as well as that of the external world. As a result, we can receive information and guidance about both realities in our dreams.

- *Dream clues: The nature of reality, the nature of dreams, the nature of earth, the nature of your business, the nature of your relationships, and the nature of your personality. Was the dream imagery vibrant and alive or dead and decaying? What season are you in?*

- *Universal symbols: trees, forests, sacred geometry, earth, leaves, plants, the elements (see below), dirt, and bodies of water.*

THE ELEMENTS

Fire, water, earth, and air are natural elements often found in many symbolic guises in our dreams. In Taoism, a fifth element is included: metal. Dreams of the elements are so important for anyone who feels they've been systemically wronged through unhealthy systems or structures (familial, cultural, etc.) because these types of dream images can overturn unhealthy ideologies by providing clarity on the issue and then offer alternative solutions. Dream images provide us with opportunities for restorative well-being, both individually and collectively.

Fire speaks to that which can burn, consume, and destroy. As a dream symbol, it often represents the dreamer's internal state of being. Perhaps you are consumed, fired up, volatile, or angry and simply need to find a healthy outlet?

Have you been burned by someone or something? Have you dreamed of an old structure burning down (old and unhelpful ideologies and beliefs being destroyed)? Ask yourself what will replace this structure of belief. Is external collective rage extinguishing your inner peace, or do you need to get fired up on behalf of the collective? Fire also has many other attributes: it can warm a home, help feed a family, and clear out diseases (for example, through controlled forest fires). Look to the dream as a whole to understand its guidance.

Water is a complex symbol that requires an in-depth dive to understand its full and potent meaning. For the sake of brevity, water can represent your emotions, your life force, and your relationship dynamics. Do you feel flooded when you are around a specific person? Do you dam up how you feel? Are you like a tsunami? Try to recall the quality of the water in your dreams and your reaction to it to decipher its meaningful guidance.

When you dream of tornadoes, hurricanes, strong winds, and air conditioners that go on the blink, you are dealing with the element of air. Air is an element that represents the "breath of life" as well as the "winds of change." Have you ever dreamed you were struggling to hold your breath under water? In other words, are submerged (repressed) emotions draining your life force? The element of air is a powerful communicator in your dreams. Air is something you can't see, but it is a vital component required for us to survive. It is a necessity, not a desire, so the related dream symbols speak to this larger motif. Ask yourself: *What do I need to sustain my life and well-being right now?*

Earth as a dream symbol can be represented in many ways, and the imagery is intrinsically linked to the theme of nature. From earthquakes to deserts, earth is all-encompassing. Earthquake dreams generally represent foundations that are unexpectedly and forcefully ripped apart. In such cases, you are being asked to adapt and survive circumstances beyond your control. Alternatively, the dream could be alerting you to weak structures (or foundational relationships) in your life that need stabilizing. As with all dream elements, it is your reaction to the dream imagery that lends further insight into what the symbols mean.

- *Dream clues: Elemental forces are intrinsically more ancient and primal than man-made symbols. There is always an implicit message of balance with the elements, so seek to ask what can be restored in your life to a better state of being.*

- *Universal symbols: A gun firing, volcanoes, being fired, candles, eternal flame, "you light my fire" (passion/eros), fireplaces, and matches. Water, rain, taps, showers, drains, waterfalls, rivers, ponds, lakes, seas, and tributaries. Man-made air symbols like airplanes, airmail, airtime, and swords. And natural air symbols like tornadoes, hurricanes, and the wind. Earth symbols are represented by dirt, coffins, trees, sandpits, quarries, gardens, canyons, mountains, and nature at large.*

MONEY

Money represents many things: security, stability, ease, comfort, luxury, poverty, frugality, and hardship. If you dream about money, it can be representative of your actual financial state of well-being, but it can also symbolize much more than that. Have you found the treasures within? Are you wealthy in spirit and heart? Are you comfortable with both receiving and giving in your relationships, work, and life in general? Dreams of money speak to your material and spiritual well-being, your security and stability, and your inner richness of character and spirit.

- *Dream clues: If you had all the money in the world, how would you behave? How do you support your community?*

- *Universal symbols: cash, bank accounts, checks, antiques, wishing wells, pomegranates, seeds, corn, pentacles, pennies, pregnancy (fertile/abundant), jewelry, shells (sand dollars), treasure, coins, gold, Bitcoin, wallets, gifts, and safe-deposit boxes.*

NAKEDNESS

It's a universal dream: somehow you find yourself completely naked in a room full of strangers. Being naked in a crowd epitomizes what it feels like to be vulnerable and uncomfortable. When you are naked, you have nothing to "hide" behind. You are simply cloaked in the essence of who you are. So if you dream of being naked in a stressful situation, it may be time to reflect on whether shame is being activated in your life.

On the other hand, if you dream of being naked in a wonderful and serene manner, the dream imagery is not congruent with the feeling of shame. The dream shows you that you are comfortable in your skin and that your social personas are not getting in the way of your well-being. You may dream of being naked in a multitude of scenarios, and each offers clues as to what you need to confront, alter, or ultimately accept.

- *Dream clues: With whom can you be your most vulnerable and authentic self?*

- *Universal symbols: the body, bodies, clothes, and newborn babies.*

SEX

Sex dreams can simply be about a physical and erotic release of tension and desire. Yet oftentimes sex dreams have nothing to do with physicality and are more symbolic in nature. Do you know the person you are sleeping with? (Are there aspects of yourself you may need to discover and revel in?) Are there many people in the dream? (Can pleasure and joy be shared more freely in your life?) What needs "unifying" in your life? Have you ever dreamed about sex with someone you never would have thought of in this context? Dreams of a sexual nature can be about the union of opposites, which may mean healing any discordant elements within you by holding two diverging thoughts or emotions at the same time.

- *Dream clues: How did you feel in the dream? What was the experience like?*

- *Universal symbols: the body.*

THE BODY

Bodies often look different or even strange in dreams. They shift and alter according to what you are experiencing in the dreamscape. If a part of your body is hurt or injured in the dream you may want to ask: *Why this specific part of my body?* If you hurt your eyes in the dreamscape, you could ask: *What am I not seeing clearly?* Alternatively, if gazing upon a dream figure hurts your eyes, who or what do they represent? Ask yourself: *Am I uncomfortable with what I am experiencing and seeing in my life? Am I blinded to the truth of the situation?*

If your hands or feet feature prominently in a dream, you may want to reflect on how well you are taking things in stride. Are you **hand**ling a waking life situation well? Alternatively, did you watch someone have a heart attack in the dreamscape? If so, ask yourself: *Where is love entirely lacking in my life?* The remedy for a broken heart is love and connection.

Themes of harmony or disharmony also can be represented via the body in dreams. For example, people often dream of teeth in varying states (healthy, rotten, broken, etc.). Teeth dreams are related to nurturance and survival because we eat to survive and our teeth are instrumental in that process. Dreams about teeth invite you to see how you are assimilating (chewing) or not assimilating (unable to chew) people, situations, and emotions in your life. In other words, are you in harmony or disharmony with elements and relationships in your life?

- *Dream clues: How did your body look and feel in the dream? Were you dreaming of your past, present, or future self? Were there masculine, feminine, or gender-neutral or non-binary elements highlighted in the dream? Are inherited stories playing a role in your life? Where can you bring more balance to your life?*

- *Universal symbols: the body or body parts.*

ILLNESS VERSUS WELLNESS

Many dream symbols are related to illness, but generally, the most common ones are hospitals, ambulances, doctors, bandages, and hurt animals. When you dream of these kinds of images, you are being invited to look at what needs healing or intervention in your life. Injuries may have nothing to do with your physical body but rather the dream may be directing your attention to a relationship dynamic or an inner conflict that needs to be addressed and changed for greater personal well-being. Implicit in dreams of illness is the message of wellness. That is an opportunity to feel better. (Look to the other dream symbols for the solutions.)

Sometimes people dream of mythic symbols related to illness or wellness, like the Rod of Asclepius (a snake wrapped around a rod). This symbol is used by many medical hospitals as well as doctors in private practices, so it is something that is often unconsciously associated with well-being. When you dream of mythic symbols, pay attention to them because they are larger than just personal symbols. They speak to fundamental shifts in states of being that are collective in nature but also relevant to your current circumstances.

- *Dream clues: How can you invite greater well-being into your life and relationships?*

- *Universal symbols: doctors, hospitals, nurses, medical machinery, and ambulances (urgent healing).*

STILLNESS VERSUS DISTURBANCES

Cars shrieking to a halt, the ground shaking beneath your feet, and dream figures that chase you down. These dream images are all disturbing to some degree—as are dreams where violence takes place. When you are disturbed by something or someone in your dreams, an element of fear leaves you feeling helpless and frightened. And so the dream imagery speaks to situations in your waking life that require active acknowledgment and healing. Ask yourself: *Where is fear playing a role in my life, and how would it be different if it weren't?*

Cars shrieking to a halt may represent you feeling like things are spinning out of control. Or a wish for things to come to a stop. (Are you feeling overwhelmed?) The ground shaking beneath your feet may mean you are not on solid footing, so double-check your foundations, paperwork, and any contractual matters.

On the opposite spectrum, where you dream of peaceful imagery, you have found the stillness within. There is a sacred place within us all that cannot be tainted by any external condition or person. Sometimes dream imagery comes to remind you of your ability to consciously find and cultivate that sacred quality of serenity and stillness in your waking life.

- *Dream clues: Does a situation or relationship in your life need better boundaries? Are you able to accept your "darker" personality traits and behaviors? How can you cultivate peace in your life? In which avenues of your life will balance and moderation help?*

- *Universal symbols: lakes, water, moon, darkness, silence, nature, cars, angelic or religious figures, and temperance.*

SHAPES

Do you feel bent out of shape? Are you squeezing yourself into a small or otherwise constricted space (a community) you don't fit into? Where can you release resistance in your life and allow more "flow"? Shapes feature in multiple ways in your dreams. Circles are universal symbols found in almost all ancient wisdom traditions that speak to the belief of reincarnation and the natural course of life. The triangle is a symbol representing the holy trinity, which at its core represents divinity. A square can symbolize foundational roots, houses, and the number four. When shapes feature prominently in your dreams, you are being invited to see things from a larger perspective, one in which you let the structure "shape" you for the better.

- *Dream clues: Why am I dreaming of this shape now?*

- *Universal symbols: squares, circles, triangles, octagons (an alternative symbol for infinity because of the associated 8), hexagons, rectangles, and crosses.*

TIME

We often dream of being in different time periods and as different versions of ourselves. How often do you dream of yourself as your current age? Do you dream of family members as they are now or as their younger or older selves? Time as a symbolic element in dreams is purposeful because it can help trigger lucidity (when you recognize you are dreaming in the actual dream) as well as help you clarify how you feel about aging, life cycles, relationships, and any other conditions in your life that are presently meaningful. If you dream of being in a different time period (say, China in the late 1800s), you may want to research historical aspects of that period to understand why you are dreaming of that specific dreamscape.

- *Dream clues: Ask yourself which version of yourself are you dreaming of, present, past, or future self?*

- *Universal symbols: watches, clocks, flowers, bell towers, cell phones, hour clocks, and sands of time as represented by a desert.*

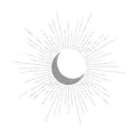

A TO Z COLLECTIVE DREAM SYMBOLS
AND THEIR POTENTIAL MEANINGS

A

Angel: The need for a higher perspective imbued with faith and belief.

Apple: Look to see what you can intentionally cultivate in your life for greater well-being and prosperity. Alternatively, are you harvesting the fruits of your labor?

Argument: Inner conflict or the need for better boundaries in relationships, as well as expressing how you really feel.

B

Beach: Finding tranquility away from everyday life. If you (or something else) are "beached," you need to acknowledge the feeling of being stranded.

Bed: "Lying" in bed indicates the need for more transparency in your intimate relationships. Or it's simply a message to rest more.

Boardwalk: A chosen path with specific consequences reflected by the state of the boardwalk. Is the boardwalk in good or poor condition?

C

Castle: An internal place of wealth and sovereignty or isolation and restriction.

Chased: Feeling anxious or stressed.

Clothing: Your identity and the social "masks" you wear and how they influence your relationships.

D

Dancing: The need for more joy and celebration in your life.

Death: Transformation from one state of being to another.

Door: A gateway to multiple and infinite possibilities—take a chance!

E

Eagle: A need for a higher perspective that includes your spiritual nature.

Eating: Assimilating thoughts, ideas, and beliefs as represented by specific food. A bitter orange can be interpreted as a bitter belief.

Electronic equipment: Being connected with others.

F

Food: The need for foundational nurturance and self-care.

Friend: Connecting to like-minded people who make you feel good. Or frenemy: groupthink or competition that has become unhealthy.

Funeral: Laying to rest a belief, relationship, or pattern.

G

Gate: Closing off something either on purpose or unintentionally.

Gift: Inner treasure offered by your psyche so you can receive more in your life.

Giving: Generosity and abundance offered in community.

H

Hospital: Focus on healing any injured or hurt aspects of yourself or your relationships.

Hotel: A desire to enjoy the more luxurious aspects of life.

House: The state of your psyche.

I

Ice: Stuck or repressed emotions that need release. Or an intentional standstill, which can help you get back on track if you use the time well.

Ice cream: A return to childhood innocence. Ask yourself if you are craving moments of sweetness in your life and then find a way to share your joy.

Island: The need for more time alone. Alternatively, feeling lonely.

J

Jail: Feeling imprisoned or punished (a sign to release guilt and shame) by a situation or person that has "authority" over you.

Job: Working at something.

Jurassic: An ancient belief that is influencing your life and behaviors.

K

Keeper: Safeguarding something valuable (the need for self-protection).

Kettle: A situation that may "boil over" if left unaddressed.

Kid: The need for childlike play and joy. If you are a parent and you dream of your kids, the dream can also be about their well-being.

L

Landscape: The current structure of your psyche.

Lighthouse: When you acknowledge your light, you become a beacon for others to do the same.

Lovers: Duality and union in your life and relationships, including the relationship you have with yourself.

M

Military: Fighting for or defending something you love. Alternatively, if you are being chased down by the army, you may feel persecuted in your life. Or are you at war with yourself?

Mirror: A reflection of beliefs that have been internalized and are now being made conscious. Or the need to immerse yourself in systems that explore higher consciousness.

Mountain: The need to summon serenity and strength for the journey ahead.

N

News: External events that are influencing your life.

Nighttime: Seeing in the dark. A message to work with your intuition and dreams.

Noise: Feeling overwhelmed in your waking life. A call to silence any superfluous aspects of your life.

O

Ocean: The unconscious and the mystery of the deep unknown.

Operation: The need for serious healing, which requires skilled or expert help. Reach out for support.

Orange: Focus on your creative

life and expressing yourself authentically.

P

People: Can represent aspects of yourself or the relationships you are in.

Pet: Unconditional love and support.

Playground: The need for more joy and fun.

Q

Queen: Owning your throne as well as the feminine aspects of yourself.

Quiet: Longing for peace and stillness.

Quilt: Weaving any disparaging elements in your life into one unified masterpiece.

R

Rest: Trusting that it is safe for you to take time for yourself.

Resurrection: Rising from the ashes. Keep on going!

Running: Avoiding an issue, feeling, or problem in your life.

S

Shower: Washing away or cleansing something that is adversely affecting you.

Sports: Playing well with others or the need to compete on behalf of a group (family).

Subway: An aspect in your subconscious that is influencing your current circumstances.

T

Time: The cycles of your life—what season are you in?

Transport: Moving from one state of being to another.

Travel: Exploring different and foreign aspects of yourself.

U

Umbrella: Being protected and sheltered in the storm. A message to be well thought out and prepared for what may come.

Under cover: Trying to hide away from something (a belief, problem, or person). The need to face what you are avoiding so you can move past the obstacle.

Under water: Exploring the unconscious facets of your mind.

V

Vacation: The need for a change of scenery.

Vet: An instinct (represented by the animal) within you is injured, and you are currently in the process of tending to it.

Violence: Inner conflict or turmoil within your partnerships.

W

Water: Your emotions, intrapsychic life, and intuition.

Well: The depth of your inner wisdom.

Whale: The great mystery.

X

X: An ex-lover. Alternatively, the letter X represents that you are about to hit your target or goal in some way.

X: An omission.

X-ray: Beyond normal vision. Try to see things from a different perspective.

Y

Yam: Familial comfort and down-to-earth pleasures or people in your life.

Yarn: Weaving a plan that will cloak you in material comfort.

Yesterday: Something in your past that is currently influencing your life or affecting you.

Z

Zebra: Seeing things in a very black-and-white manner (all-or-nothing thinking). The need for a greater, more inclusive perspective.

Zipper: Concealing or revealing intimate details about yourself (feeling vulnerable).

Zoo: Psychological instincts that have been compartmentalized.

Zoom: Feeling like things are happening very fast. Or interconnectivity through technology and how that influences you.

HOW I FELT IN MY DREAM

- Nurtured, secure, peaceful, loved
- Creative, cheerful, fired up, happy
- Energetic, excited, joyful
- Trusting, confident, certain
- Positive, optimistic, eager
- Encouraged, trusting, happy
- Satisfied, serene, accepted, hopeful
- Dull, bored, indifferent
- Cynical, distrusting, pessimistic
- Thwarted, agitated, irritated, frazzled
- Tender, unsettled, nervous, panicked

- Sad, discouraged, let down, upset
- Apprehensive, concerned, hesitant
- Afraid, anxious, frightened
- Bitter, blamed, resentful
- Deterred, unsettled, dissatisfied
- Hostile, angry, hurt, in pain
- Retaliatory, vengeful
- Enraged, disgusted, abhorrent, hateful
- Envious, inadequate, jealous
- Ashamed, self-conscious, afraid, unworthy
- Fearful, dreadful, terrorized

FEELINGS AND THOUGHTS ON ALL THE DREAM THEMES UNCOVERED IN THIS JOURNAL

This space is dedicated to helping you reflect on all the dream themes that have appeared throughout your dream-journaling process. It is helpful to do this reflection only after this journal is full. Simply scroll through all the checklists and note all the themes that repeat. These themes are psychologically insightful and will point you in the direction of wholeness and well-being. It's also a wonderful experience to scroll through multiple dream journals to look back and see how you've progressed through all the different periods (and themes!) of your life.

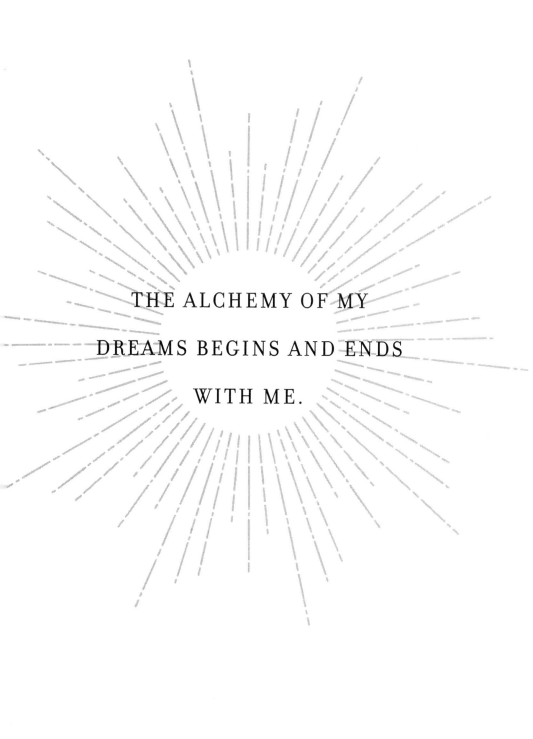

THE ALCHEMY OF MY
DREAMS BEGINS AND ENDS
WITH ME.

ABOUT THE AUTHOR

Athena Laz is a depth psychologist and dream guide. She also is the author of *The Alchemy of Your Dreams: A Modern Guide to the Ancient Art of Lucid Dreaming and Interpretation.*

Athena's work merges spiritual wisdom with practical psychological know-how. Thousands of people worldwide have enjoyed her courses, membership program, and retreats.

For more information, please visit athenalaz.com or find her online @athena_laz.

Also by

ATHENA LAZ

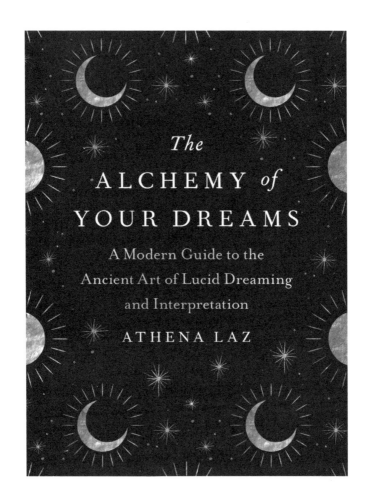

tarcherperigee